A Woman of Great Faith

Apostle Doctor
Florene Vick Jones

Table of Contents

Introduction

Apostle Dr. Florene Vick Jones:
A woman of wisdom, discerner, prayer warrior, appointed, anointed, called, and ordained by God as overseer of the Ministry's Administration, a mother; is called Spiritually Mother, will see and hear prophecies from God to teach and preach all that, and loves God because she is holy, saved, and obedient in the labor of the Gospel of Christ.

Married to one man: Jesus Christ, one good groom. She walks in the direction of Christ's love, of the call of God who receives her as a woman of God who is very careful of the anointed that God has placed in her life. "She is not jealous and she greets you as the woman the Spirit that is holy, holy, holy; carrying the five-fold gifts and talent in the perfecting of ministry." (Ephesians 4:11-12)

The utmost then and now is a calling, not a title. Sound doctrine is the call of God under authority of Jesus. God speaks wisdom, knowledge, and understanding.

Dr. Florene V. Jones has experience in pastorship, leadership, administration, servant watchman, direction, church management, and pulpit and stage lighting. The salt of the earth is a stone; a rock that Jesus built.

Apostle Florene is a Doctor in Biblical Studies, is a counselor and a substitute teacher in the Wake County Public School System. She is also grandmother to six grandchildren and six great-grandchildren. She is trustworthy, loyal, faithful, long-suffering, honorable, educated apostle and discerner has fellowship in Ministries Helpmeet in the Community. She is a virtuous woman who carries the word of God; charged to Praise and thankful to God for all fasting workmen. She is an ambassador and officer on all calls.

Walking and do operate in the Spirit dedicated. You can find this woman, Florene V. Jones, in the beginning (Genesis) and in the ending (Revelations). Amen.

"Don't worry about anything; instead, pray about everything. Tell God what you need and thank him for all he has done"
(Philippians 4:6 NLT)

First Phase: The Foundation of Faith

Chapter One: Dreams of Becoming Something

My name is Florene Vick Jones.

I am writing this book and dedicating it to my family to let them know how much I love them. Also, so that they can read and see how much a person can accomplish when they have God on their side. There is no secret that God can't help you get through. I have always wanted to be somebody. While growing up I would always tell my parents that one day I will be somebody. I said it so much, one day my Mother said, "I sure hope I live long enough to see that day come." Trust me, God let her live to see it. And by faith, I was able to live to see my dream come true.

It takes prayer and fasting for a person to hold out to see what they have been dreaming about to come to pass. With God's help, I was able to hold out and see it take place. It took patience and all I had to offer to continue to make sure that, before God calls me home, I myself could see and read my book; what God had allowed me to publish. I want my children to be proud of me, because if they don't have the courage, time, and patience to do something in their life, then somebody had to do it. This book will help them along the way when things get hard for them in raising their children. They can look and read what their Mother went through to raise them. Without God, you can't do much of anything. But with God, all things are possible. No one has to tell me what I already know without a shadow of doubt. My life is put into this book and with God's help I hope it will help someone along the way. Please travel with me as I continue to write this book.

This book is based on a true story about my late husband and my children. What a grand time we had when we all were growing up together. I tell people I grew up with my children and that helped me to look young. My husband Cleveland and I were married at the age of eighteen and went to the same school which was Spaulding High School in Spring Hope, N.C. They were the good old days especially when you look back and see where you came from. Well let me get into the book so you can journey down through Flo and Clint's love lane. I hope you will be inspired when you read my book. To God be the glory.

In a small town named Zebulon, N.C., lived a young girl named Florene Vick. She was born to a man named George Cleveland Vick and a lady named Leora Barnes Vick. This happened on November 14, 1943. Florene was very precious most of the time. She would read, write, and play by herself; not that she didn't mingle with her other brothers and sisters because she did but just knew how far to go with them. Florene had eight siblings beside herself. That was a large family back in those days. Growing up, I would always tell my mother I wanted to be somebody. That was a dream I had

for myself. As time went on I strived to follow my
dream.

Chapter Two:
Paths to Love & Marriage

I attended two schools as I began to grow older. One was Jones Hill Elementary School in Nash County and the other one was Spaulding High School in Spring Hope N.C. I went to Jones Hill my early years of school from first grade through the sixth grade. I failed the first grade because I loved my Mother so much that I didn't want to leave her. After that first year I failed the first grade, I began to think about my dream. I wanted to be somebody and I reached for it. After that, I got myself together, went to school, and never failed another grade.

I started at Spaulding High School when I was in the sixth grade and worked hard. I got in everything I could that the school had to offer. My parents were sharecroppers so you know they didn't make much money doing that type of work. At least we had a place to stay, food to eat, and clothes to put on our back. During the time of farming, I had to stay home and help work in the field with my parents. That caused me to miss days out of school. I still held on to my dream. I wanted to be somebody. As time went on, some of my sisters and brothers began to move on with their lives like leaving home and getting married and starting their families. That left only a few of us at home to help my parents on the farm.

I still held on to my dream. I wanted to be somebody. By the time I reached middle school, I could see things come in play of what I wanted out of life. My teacher saw what I was looking at for myself. When there were days I had to stay out of school and work on the farm, one of my teachers, who was my physical education teacher Mr. Henderson, would collect all of my school work from my other teachers and bring them to me.

One day, I was working on the farm. I believe I was chopping tobacco and my brother said, "Look Florene, I believe your teacher is coming to see you. Looks like he has some papers in his hand." It was my physical education teacher. So he came up and introduced himself to my mother and father and told them the reason he was there. My Dad said, "We will try not to keep her out no more than I have to." That is then when my parents realized that I had a dream. That one day I would be somebody. As time went on, I joined the Glee Club, Student Council, Basketball; anything I could do, I did it. As time went on and I got older, I had made such a good impression with my teachers. By the time I had gotten to the eighth grade I really was moving up the ladder. I could be out working on the farm and my teacher would vote me in to do something to help my class. When I return back to school, my classmates would tell me that I was voted in to be on the Student Council.

I would go and sit in the hallway in the high school and take names of the people who would be late coming to class. After that, I would be called out of my classroom to go and sub for two first-grade teachers for them to go to meetings or attend to personal business. All the time God was working behind the scene. After saying all of that, there was a young man that had his eyes on me because he lived not too far from where I lived and my older brother was married to his aunt. Even though he was not the only one that was looking, all I wanted was to be somebody. As time went on and I was getting older, it was getting to be dating time and this person made sure he got the first chance to have a date with one of the popular girls at school. So what he would do, he would come to my house and help my younger brother gather wood for the house. In those days we had wood heaters, no central heat and air.

You know the old saying "get in with the parents and you will have a chance at what you are trying to do." He really worked that puzzle so he knew he had it made with the boys at the time. But I knew I would have a hard time by the way I carried myself. I always dressed neat and clean; everything in its proper place. Most guys would be interested in a person like that. But the guy played his cards straight. He got in with my parents and that was all he needed to do. Also, I had a younger brother so that just made things better for him. He would come to my house to help my younger brother cut wood for the house, feed the pigs and the chickens, pick cucumbers; whatever the job calls for, he would help.

My father would call him "my boy" as time went on, and my parents told me I could start dating and I tried to date other boys. This person could not handle it so well. I just wanted to be friends and nothing else. All I wanted was to be somebody. I had two cousins in prison and I would write to them and say encouraging words to them. That made them feel real good. They would send me money and pictures that they had drawn of me. My mother kept one picture for a long time but something happened to it and she couldn't find it. I have always been a person who thought about others as well as myself. I said that to say this, even though this person couldn't handle what he was looking at, I had to let him know if he was going to be my friend. He would have to be understanding, acceptable, controlling, and help me to pursue what my dream was: to be somebody.

This person felt like that was asking for way too much, so I had to show him. I started dating other guys; just having fun and that was all. Every time this person would see me out with someone else, he was ready to fight. I really didn't like that spirit, but all I could do was pray. He wasn't the one I really wanted to date regularly. I didn't want to date anyone regularly; just a young girl who had a lot going on for herself and too much time. Well, time went on and when he saw how things were going before he would be a loser, I guess he thought through how he could trap me.

So he would get his father's car, come to where I would be, and try to start a fight with whomever I would be with. That way, they would leave me and he could be the one to take me home. Then he would take me to some woods and make me have sex with him. I would cry and go home and tell my parents, but they seem to act as if I had not said a word about anything. I even told my father he was not the boy he thought he was. My father wanted me to go deeper into what I was trying to tell him. So I did. My father told him that if he got me pregnant, he sure as hell would have to take care of it. He didn't care what it took for him to do it but he could count on it.

Sometimes I wonder if teenage girls try to talk to their parents about problems, they want to play it off? They should take it in stride and do as my father did. Even though it still happened to me, I felt like my life would never be the same. But I really turned to God to help me through what I had to go through.

Chapter Three:
Joys & Sorrows of Motherhood

I had just turned seventeen and was hoping to graduate and pursue my education. I did, but not the way it should have been. I had a little girl and she was precious to the both of us. My world crashed and all I could do was pray. He dropped out of school in the eleventh grade and got a job in Raleigh working in a grocery store making thirty-seven dollars a week.

He lived with his sister so he had to pay some money. How much, I never knew. He would come home every two weeks. I lived with my parents in Spring Hope, N.C. and his parents lived there, too, but they did not try to help with the supplies for the baby at all. He had to do everything. But that is what you get when you want to be so bad. All I could do was pray and watch God work. I waited until I was eighteen and we got married on March 5, 1962 in a little town named Nashville, N.C. My Mother got sick and God let me know what her problem was.

She told me I was too young to try to raise a child by myself. I told her I had to learn some time and staying there was not helping me. I need to be where my husband was. The next week he came home, I told him I was ready to come to Raleigh and live. At the time, he was still living with his sister in a rooming house with a little old lady. I had a sister and her family lived in Raleigh, N.C., also. She came home and told me I could come and stay with her and her family and she would help me with the baby. That is how Raleigh got to be my home until today.

After the move, I was able to stay home and work with my little girl. Nine months later I had another little girl. My hands were really full, so one day my younger brother came to Raleigh. By that time, my husband had gotten another job making much more money than what he was making so he was able to get my brother on with him. The company was Wonder Bread. That did help out a lot. So one day my brother had a day off, he went looking for another place for us to live. He found a three-bedroom apartment not too far from my sister and her family. So we moved and he moved in with us. He worked hard and helped us out a lot.

All of us were in the three-bedroom apartment together. It all worked out for the good. One weekend we went with my Sister and her Husband to visit our family. I left the oldest daughter with my mother and father and brought the youngest one back with me. Just before we got into Raleigh, my brother-in-law hit two big mules and that took us down an embankment. My baby was thrown out of my arms and into some bushes. All I could hear was her crying. We had to look through the bushes to find her. Glass was everywhere; all in her face, hair, clothes. She had a lot of hair so you can imagine what a time we had getting all of that glass out of her hair. I was so hurt about my baby. She and I were the only ones to get hurt. We were taken to WakeMed and got treated and released the same night. All I could do was pray, "God, please do not let anything happen to my baby. As a matter of fact, do not let harm come to either one of us." My mouth was messed up in the front and all of my teeth were knocked back in my mouth. After a couple of weeks, I went to see a doctor. He started to treat my mouth so he could start pulling out what had to come out.

It was a time for a while. As soon as I thought things were getting better, my little girl got sick. She could not keep her milk down. She would spit it back up. I called my mother after two days went by. She said, "Bring her home and we will take her to the doctor and see what he has to say." My husband had a friend who lived not too far from my mother and father, so he asked him if he would take me and my mother to take the baby to the doctor. My mother and I went to the doctor with the baby and the doctor said that by her losing so much fluid, I would need to take her to the hospital to get some fluid and I could bring her back after it was over. She stayed three days and on the third night, she said goodbye to me. She went to be with the Lord. From that day until this day, I was never told by the doctor what my baby's problem was.

My mother said diverticulitis because it brought blood instead of stool. If I knew then like I know now, I would have given them a run for their money.

After losing my little girl, I was so disappointed I felt like I had lost everything. She was such a beautiful little girl. She was five months old in her passing. Just got to where she knew everybody and so playful. My Father would watch her for me to go and take care of business. After a few years had passed, I went to the family Doctor and he told my mother if I didn't have another child she would not have me long.

My mother called and asked me to come home; so I did and she told me what the Doctor had said. She told me "God did what he had to do and was nothing no one could do about it." And the sooner I accept it the better off I would be. I started to look at the little girl I had left for me to cherish and love. At first all I could do was question God what did I do for him to do that to me. Never got an answer; I began to seek God the more. After four years had passed I got pregnant again and had an 8lbs. and 12ounce son. I thought to myself God gave me back a daughter and a son all in one. The reason I said that is to say this: I didn't weigh but 98lbs. myself and to have a son that big made the difference what I lost. He is all grown up and no kids of his own. Just an all around Son that loves

his family and works hard to accomplish goals in
his life.

Chapter Four:
Awakening to Ministry

We were in a Pentecostal Holiness Church and we had church every Sunday, every Sunday night, and every Wednesday night, and still find time to go home and check on our family. While we were in the church, I started working with the young people in the church which weren't but five starting out. As time went on just as anything else, the young people department started to grow and the harder I worked the harder the young people began to work. Within twelve months' time, the young people department went like a whirlwind. I knew by then I was on my way to the top. God started working in my life so strong, there were nothing for me to do but say, "Thank you, Lord." By then, we were about twenty-five people in the young people department. I started a young adult choir with those people, and the church went up in flames behind that choir.

Every year, we would have a choir anniversary. I would pick out patterns and let the choir look at them and decide which one they wanted and I would get one of the mothers to make whatever they picked out. The guys would pattern behind the girls. When we stepped out, we were together and looking good. We made the choirs that came to our anniversary sick by the way we were dressed. All I could say was, "Search me O God and know my heart; my heart is your heart, my eyes are your eyes, my hands are your hands." We travelled the East Coast singing and praising God. The choir got so good my husband began to sing with us.

There was peace like a river in my life. I was so glad that God had smiled on me. After a while as time went on, I had a youth revival at the church and the young man who was conducting the revival called me out one night and told me he wanted to talk to me after the service was over. At that time, I was pregnant with the fourth child. I was carrying her so low I had to sit on a pillow to be comfortable. So when the young man told me that, I said, "God, not again. Have I got to go through something with this child? If so, I know you are with me and you will see me through." After church, he came and told me that "something good and something bad were going to happen to me but the good would overpower the bad."

For real, it happened to me. My little girl was born premature. She was due December 10 but she came September 12, 1975, and was born at Rex Hospital Raleigh, N.C. She stayed from September 12 until November 25, 1975. That was the best Thanksgiving I had ever had because she came home the day before Thanksgiving. She weighed 2 lbs. 7 and a half oz. and lost 5 and a half ounces after she was born. I have to let you know, nothing happened to my little girl. That was what the young man was talking about; the good would outweigh the bad.

She is now forty years old and has three children of her own. They are fourteen, ten, and nine. See what prayer can do. After going through all of that in 1975, I was called into the ministry by God, not by man. I went forth on Psalm Sunday night at 7:30 p.m. and I was told by my mother and sister that fifty souls were saved that night. I went out like a light baptized in the Holy Ghost. It was the next day when I came around, I didn't know anything about what had happened. All I could remember was telling the people my theme of my message, "Let not your heart be troubled." A few words after that and that was all I could remember. After my initial sermon, I was made the youth minister over the youth department.

I stayed with the church for two years, and all the time I was praying for God to let me go home and help my family. God answered my prayer. I left the Pentecostal Holiness Church and went to my hometown in Spring Hope, N.C. I met with the pastor and his wife and told them what God had said I could do. They would always come on every fourth Sunday just to hear me speak and the choir sing. When I told him what had happened, he said he had prayed and asked God to send him somebody like me to help him in his church. He said, "I didn't know it would be you." He said, "I might have some problems with your Pastor if I say come on and help me."

I told him if God said everything was final. So I went home, joined Pleasant Hill Holiness Church in Spring Hope, N.C., and went to work. Reverend Wilkins had only three young people in his church. With prayer, you can do a lot. I started out with this three, and added to the church my nieces, nephews, my husband, my brother, and came up with another twenty-five voice choir for his church. We, as a family church, really made Reverend Wilkins and First Lady Sarah very proud and thankful for letting me come down to work in the church.

Reverend Wilkins pushed me all the way to the top of the ministerial board as far as my licenses were concerned. I received my Lay License, Ministry License, Evangelist License, and my Pastoral License. Then I went out to start a church. God led me to the Young Woman Christian Association and that was where I started my church. It was open in 1984-2003. I moved from there to the Chavis Community Building for two years and left there and went to New Market Drive for three years and in 2010 I asked God to let me go back out in the field. I set up under Bishop Benjamine Williams for one year and a half and God answered my prayer.

In 1995 I lost my husband but I kept on moving for the Lord. Now that I am back out on the field, I have a prayer breakfast every first Saturday morning at The Golden Carrol. I also have a Women's Conference every year at different places. This year will make the fourth year; it comes from the Woman of the Bible. The first year was just a conference. The second year it came from the Book of Esther; how she stood up for her people and won favor from the King. The third year it came from the book of Ruth; how she bonded with her mother-in-law Naomi. This year, it will come from the book of Deborah which is called a "Bee" and a Fearless Woman.

In my closing, I would like to say, "God gives wisdom, knowledge, and joy to those who please Him." Ecclesiastes 2:26. May God be the glory.

Second Phase
Renewal & Resilience

Chapter Five:
A Second Chance of Healing

This is starting the second phase of my life. My oldest daughter was working on this job along with about thirty-five more people and the man who was their supervisor was one of Uncle Sam's man. She said one day he asked her who was in her family who is a minister. She in turn said, "My mother." Then she asked him why he asked her that question. That was when he told her that he was a seventeen-year alcoholic and he had tried everything to try to stop because he had messed up two marriages, and in each marriage he had a daughter.

He told my daughter he had a sister who went to school to learn to preach, but she was not called by God. My daughter told him, "My mother was called, appointed, anointed, and was equipped for the journey." He in turn told her, "It was written on her." So one day I was on my job working and I received a phone call and it was from my daughter. She began to tell me a little bit about him. I never gave it a thought that my child had so much faith in me. I began to pray as she would tell me things he would say to her and her cousin as they worked. So these are the words I would say to myself, "Show me your ways, Lord. Teach me your paths. Guide me in your truth and teach me for you are God my Savior and my hope is in you all day long" (Psalm 25:4–5 NIV).

The reason I said those words was because I knew she would get around to asking me to help him. She had seen me go up against some tough situations. And every time, God would bring me out. Not bragging or complaining, I really had to have God in order to do whatever the job calls for. "The blessing of the Lord makes one rich, and He adds no sorrow with it." Proverbs 10:22 (NKJV) It happened just like I said and thought. So when the day came and she asked me to help him, I turned her down. She couldn't believe I had done that. I guess, as she had time to sleep on it, she called me back the next day and said to me, "You mean to tell me you can't help this person but you help others?" Good question. I thought at the time I didn't want to get involved because I was at a turning point in my life.

Not for the worst, it was just that I had so much going on with me, I just felt like I needed to cry out to someone myself. I remember reading in Numbers 6:24–26 (NKJV), "The Lord bless you and keep you; the Lord make His face shine upon you and be gracious to you; The Lord lift up His countenance upon you and give you peace." That wording would help me get through whatever I had to face. She didn't give in or give up. She was really concerned about this person's soul. She wouldn't let go. So finally I gave in and told her I would meet him but couldn't promise her anything. She said, "Just meet him, Mama. I know you can do whatever it takes. I have seen you do a lot by the help of the Lord."

I am not bragging or complaining but when I went out, I knew I would win because I would pray and get my answer from God; that was all I needed to do, what I had to do. So I gave in and told her I would meet with him. And when the day came, I met with him and I saw him from a distance. I could see right through him. I knew he was what she said he was. One thing I liked about him was how he gave respect right off. That was the first thing I noticed about him. That is one of the things I demand: respect. I tell my children that all the time. I am sure they will get tired of hearing that word.

Not only was he respectful, he also knew what to do when we went to eat so we could talk. I went to sit down at the table and he was right there to pull the chair out for me so I could sit down. I told him that I never got that from my husband. I told him my husband was a good man, but most of his time was spent working; that he had two jobs, so much time was spent away from home. I had my children to take care of so it really didn't bother me. Then when we got on his case, I listened to what he had to say. Then I asked him was he saved, he answered me and said "No, but whatever it takes for me to be saved, I am willing to do so." I in turn invited him to come to church with me on Sunday and we would see what God would do for him.

It took more than one Sunday, but God touched him and he was a changed man. But you know as well as I do that when you try to make a change, everything starts coming your way. And being a new convert, he didn't have the power to get rid of it. But He was sincere so God helped him out. "Worry weighs a person down; an encouraging word cheers a person up" (Proverbs 12:25 NLT). As time went on, he came to church every Sunday. He was very helpful to do all he could do. I didn't have to worry about how I would get my bags to the car, he would take them, put them in the car for me, and then help me get into the car. I went crazy because my first husband didn't do that. I had to do all of that and some more. After working with him and seeing how God was blessing, my feelings began to change. I believed he felt it before I did. He told me one Sunday that I didn't have to suffer, he would help me. I, at the time, was so wrapped up in the church I passed it by.

I was just thankful that I had some help. The church was made up of family. I had to tell them everything that I needed to get done. But with him, he just picked up and did it. "God did not give us a spirit of fear, but of power and of love and of a sound mind." 2 Timothy 1:7 (NKJV) We continue on with the church working hard; making sure all we did was for the Lord. So one day he said to me,

"Do you think I would make you a good husband?" I was flattered. In other words, I didn't know what to say. But I finally said to him, "You might but I am spoiled. My husband spoiled me. If you think you can handle that, then you might." He in turn said, "I am willing to try." I have always heard my mother say "if you don't succeed at first, try again" if that means anything to whoever reads my book. What I took it to be was that God gives us chances after chances to see what we would do.

So why can't we give people a chance? I might be wrong but that is the way I took it. Finally, I gave him the chance to prove himself and he did a superb job. We got married and was married for thirteen years, and the last three years the devil stepped in. I think what happened was that people like family get jealous of the way I was treated and started to speak things about our marriage. For instance, he had two wives from previous marriages and a daughter in each one. So by that, if you feel like you didn't get the treatment when you had him, no one else would get it. So the relationship began to come in play and it was more than he could handle because he loved his daughters and often had to fight to keep from going to jail so he started back to drinking and smoking.

Everywhere, he would hide his liquid bottles out of the house. God would let me find them. I wouldn't say a word. I would pull them out and let him know in that way that I knew what he was doing.

Chapter Six:
Shadows & Seperation

After a period of time, it just got worse and I began to pray, "God, please help me to get out of this marriage before someone gets hurt." So one morning in the year of 2002, I was sitting in the family room of our beautiful home that God had shown me in my first marriage. It was Doctor Vick's old home in a little town called Selma, NC. God spoke to me and said, "As of this day, you will get out of this marriage."

I forgot I had asked Him to help me get out. The Spirit said, "You have been hurt enough, and enough is enough." I had three weeks to go before I got my Chaplain License. I was able to finish and God walked me through so I could get my divorce. You just can't beat God's blessing any way you try. I moved from Selma back to Raleigh with my baby daughter and her husband and family until my divorce was final then I moved out by myself. "The scripture gives us hope and encouragement as we wait patiently for God's promises to be fulfilled. My God, who gives this patience and encouragement, help you live in complete harmony with each other." Romans 15:4–5 (NLY)

I moved on while still pastoring in my Church and never looked back. He went his way and I went my way. God is still in the blessing plan. I thank God there were no children in this marriage. Everything went smoothly because God's hands were in it through it all. He is still living in Raleigh, and so am I. We never see each other and that is a good thing. I really loved that man. And he loved me. But Satan knows a person's weak spot. And that is what he works with. Who knows what might happen if we meet again. Know that the Lord your God, He is God the faithful. God who keeps his covenant and mercy for a thousand generations with those who love Him and keep His commandments (Deuteronomy 7:9 NKJV). This ends with love. "For God so loved the world that he gave his only begotten son, that whosoever believed in him should not perish, but have everlasting life" (John 3:16).

Third Phase
Divine Paths & Liberation

Chapter Seven:
A Divine Union

"Heaven and earth will pass away but my words will by no means pass away" (Matthew 24:35 NKJV). I started this out with the word of God because God put this marriage together. On September 13, 2011, God spoke into my Spirit and said he was giving me a husband. I had just been in my town house for eight months; just started to feel comfortable being in it. I didn't know what to do. I cried; I prayed. It was just a bad day for me. I had a one day job at Hospice of Wake County stuffing envelopes with letters that needed to be mailed out to doctors. That happened on the day I had to go to work. I was no good but I went to work anyway. I tried to stay but I couldn't. I had to leave and come home.

On my way home, I asked God again who was the husband that he was giving to me. Just before I got to exit onto the street to my house, God spoke and told me who he was. You know I lost it. All I could do was say, "God not that man. Anybody but that man." God in turn said, "Why not that man? He had been helping you all the time." Then I thought about how he would let us use his equipment when we would have a big service coming off. I didn't feel like I had to marry him because of that. And what made it so bad was I was told by God to call him. It was bad enough knowing what I had to do and then call him and tell him what God said. That is why I put the scripture in the beginning of this phase of my life. I called him and told him what God had said and it was a shock to him just as it was to me. The words that came from his mouth was, "If God said it, there is nothing for me to do but what he said." I thought he would have said, "I just got out of a marriage, I am not ready to get into another one." But his answer was different than what I thought it would be. I felt like I was trapped. I know God is too wise to make a mistake. I just settled down and tried to pray for guidance in what to do and which way to go. After a few days had passed, God spoke and said, "Whatever you do, do it quickly."

This was September, and on November 26 we were walking down the aisle of the church before God and everybody to get married. God showed up and showed out. That was a Holy Ghost wedding. Everybody who attended said they had never been to a wedding with so much Spirit in it. The talk went on for days about the wedding. "The Lord is righteous in all His ways and faithful in all He does." Psalm 145:17 (NIV) After the wedding, I moved out of my town house and moved in with my husband. He lived in a town house, also. His was a lot bigger than mine but not as homey. After the move, I hated that I had left my home. It was very lonesome; no one to talk to, couldn't see anyone but the people who were going and coming that lived in the complex. Where I lived there were families with children and a playground right in front of where I lived. I could sit out and look at the children play at the playground. I would walk in the afternoon and some of the children would walk with me.

My place was more family-like living where I lived at. So after a few months, I began to pray and asked God to make a way that we could move to some other place that didn't seem so gloomy. I believe God heard my cry. I went to see my brother one day and he told me about a three-bedroom house around the corner from him and gave me the man's card. So when I got back home, I called the man but it took three phone calls before he answered me back.

Then we made arrangements to meet and discuss about the house. I fell in love with the house as soon as we walked through it. My husband wasn't with me on the first walk-through. So we met again and he came and met me there and that was when we came to a conclusion about the payments. Everything went good until we moved in and all hell broke loose. He started staying out at night, later than he used to and sometimes all night. But I didn't let it bother me because I was wrapped up in my Lord and Savior Jesus Christ.

Chapter Eight:
Trials in Marriage & Ministry

As time went on, he got worse. So finally I told him, if he kept that up he could stay out and I was going to tell the church what he was doing. Then he started coming home like someone with good sense. I couldn't figure out what was going on with that picture. I didn't lose sleep over the matter. The thing that got me was that he was calling himself an apostle and that is the highest calling in Christ Jesus. How can a person be an apostle and don't know how to treat his wife? Much prayers were needed in his case. I prayed to the best of my knowledge to God to help me in what he had put me in.

"The Scripture gives us hope and encouragement as we wait patiently for God's promises to be fulfilled. My God who gives this patience and encouragement help you live in complete harmony with each other" (Romans 15:4–5). As time went on, the church was going down. No one was hardly coming, so I jumped back in and started working really hard inviting churches to come and give us a service. Then the church started to pick up every time God would start blessing. He would allow Satan to come in. There were a lot of jealousy, envy, and strife in him, so that caused the church not to grow. Then he started bringing family in who were not saved, and holding positions in the church that they shouldn't have been doing. I just couldn't go along with all of that. They were able to tell him what to do, but he couldn't listen to what I was telling him.

I have twenty-four years of experience in administration with the ministry; he only had twelve. I think he felt little because of that. God looks at the heart, not the time. It got a tad too much for me and I stood aside and let him have his church. After a couple of months, God spoke to me and said, "I made you his helpmeet and you go back and stand. I gave you power over the enemies and the world can do you no harm." I went back and did what God told me to do and everything fell back in place. After that, God allowed sickness to come up on him. First, it started with his right eye. He awoke one morning and his eye was swollen. I started putting eyedrops in his eyes. After about a couple weeks, his left leg and foot started to swell. He made it almost to the last week in July 2015 and he said God told him to turn the church over to me.

I had to pray some more and question God to see if it was true. At the time I thought he was trying to tie me down. I went along with the installation service. It was held on the third Sunday in July at 3:00 p.m. and not a family member out of his family nor my family was there. I had planned to baptize my grandchildren and great-grandchildren on that Sunday morning. We went to the pool and no one showed up, so my husband, myself, and another ministry friend baptized each other. My great-grandchildren were home from Florida; that was the reason I wanted to do the baptism. Nevertheless, I went on in the name of Jesus. My husband went in the hospital on July 31st and came out three weeks later with his left foot cut in three places: one on the side, one cross that cut, and a hole under the bottom of his foot.

I was hoping God would talk to him as to why he was down, but if he did I couldn't tell. He was out of work for three and a half months and everything fell on me. I took it and walked with it. Praying all the time, I never got a "thank you" or "I love you for what you are doing to help me." But when the day came when he was able to get up and start getting out, I knew in my spirit I was out of that house. But I still waited on God. When I heard him say on my birthday celebration that I could go if I wanted to, I started making my connection in which direction I was going.

On December 31st, I was moving out and never looked back. You can't make a marriage work if there is no love and no respect. The songwriter said "What's love got to do with it?" I tell you one thing: love makes the world go around. A dog got sense enough to know that. If they are mistreated, they will leave and go someplace else where they are loved and stay until death do them part. The same goes for people. "Love is patient, love is kind. It does not envy, it does not boast, it is not proud. It is not easily angered; it keeps no record of wrongs. It always protects, always trusts, always hopes, always perseveres" (1 Corinthians 13: 4-5, 7 NIV).

Chapter Nine:
Freedom, Reflection, & Legacy

I hope whoever reads my book that they will gather from all I have written. That Jesus is the answer for the world today. Above Him, there is no other. Jesus is the way. No matter how you are treated by somebody else, always remember: love covers a multitude of sin.

I am still preaching and tell men, women, boys, and girls that the wage of sin is death, but the gift of God is eternal life. The first name God gave me for my church was "Crusaders Holiness Church." As time went on, in the year 2000, God changed the name of the church to "Crusaders International Church of God." The church is still standing because I am standing.

I would like to thank my children: Annett J. Bullock (Christopher), Cleveland Jones Jr. (Jacklyn), and Stephanie J. Williams (Frankie) for all of their support during my time of working with them. They kept the faith and held on to God's unchanging hand while I was going through my journey in the marriages.

To God be the glory,

Apostle Doctor Florene Vick Jones

I got my Doctor in Biblical Studies and I feel like I should put more inferences on the word more than feelings and problems. But that is what makes me be the woman I am today. Without trials and tribulations you will never amount to anything. So that is why when you go through so much in life, that is when you can truly say "For God I live and for God I die" because you know what you have been through and who was the one that brought you out. Matthew 3:2, "The kingdom of heaven is at hand." People that had rejected John and at every step had opposed Jesus were insinuating that His mission had failed.

"Not with outward show"

Jesus answers, "The Kingdom of God cometh not with outward show neither shall they say, 'Lo here!' or 'Lo there!' for behold, the Kingdom of God is within you." In other words, you don't have to look for Him. The kingdom of God begins in the heart. Look not here or there for manifestation of earthly power to mark God's coming for he is already here. After the disciples had received the outpouring of the baptism of the Holy Spirit upon them, then they believed. It was not until after Christ ascended to His father and the outpouring of the Holy Spirit upon the believers that the disciples fully appreciated the Savior's character and mission. So that tells me they didn't believe until they saw with their own eyes.

I am so glad that I didn't have to wait until I was filled to believe. I always knew there was a God because I had to pray to someone and somebody.

And not just pray for no reason at all. The songwriter says "What a friend we have in Jesus all our sins and griefs to bear. What a privilege it is to carry everything to God in prayer! O what peace we often forfeit. O what needless pain to bear, all because we do not carry everything to God in prayer." I love to use songs in my messages when I am speaking because songs have a lot of meaning as well as a sermon.

After studying the different scriptures in the Bible, it strengthens my heart. I came to realize all I had been missing because I was reading and not studying. What I'm trying to say is that studying the word gets you so much out of it. It looks like God just opened you up to receive whatever you are looking for. Then after finding what you need, you just feel so blessed. I feel like a million-dollar lady. I just feel so blessed. If I had put more time in studying the word more, I feel like I would have been a better preacher, evangelist, and prophetess in all the good works. It is all good. God still loves me and gave me the wisdom, knowledge, and understanding of what He wanted me to do.

I would like to say to the readers who will take the time to read my book: Please don't beat yourself up if things don't work for you. For instance, life itself. I always say life is a gamble; some win and some lose. But nevertheless, if you hang in there you will be so glad you did. What I went through in my marriages: the first one, I had to learn to love because I felt like my dream had been blown out of proportion. The second, I was really in love with him. And the third one, I didn't know anything about him but church; not even a thought about love. But "a woman of great faith" stepped out on God's word and never thought about having anything to go through because I knew God was with me.

So I say to that: Don't give up; just keep the faith and keep looking. You will find what you are looking for; don't give up. Some people have four or five marriages before they find their soulmate, because they didn't give up. But for me, it will have to be God to speak to me again; not me on my own. All I am saying in my book "Tell the truth and shame the devil." No one likes the truth, but I am free and plan to stay that way.

The songwriter says "I am free. I am free, no longer bound. No chains holding me. My soul is resting. It's just a blessing. Praise the Lord, I am free." To all of those who long to find love that lasts, to those who just want a real, truthful, and practical dialogue on how to navigate through the curious path of dating, mating, and relating, keep looking. My book of my life is "A Woman of Great Faith." Hopefully I've said something to help you through whatever situation you are facing. Jesus said, "You will know the truth and the truth will set you free."

Dealing with love, I always have to go back to what the songwriter says "Love lifted me, love lifted me; when nothing else could help, love lifted me. You know it was love lifted me; love lifted me when nothing else could help love oh love lifted me."

Love is so important in whatever you are trying to do. If it wasn't, I don't think God would have given His only begotten Son for you and I. But He did. John 3:16 said that "For God so loved the world He gave His only begotten son that whosoever believe in Him should not perish, but have everlasting life." The songwriter picked it up and said "Everlasting life everlasting life, everlasting life is free. I am so glad Jesus gave it to me; everlasting life is free." Love began with you celebrating life by realizing at the center of your world stands the "love of your soul"-the one who created love, the one who loves you more than anyone else ever can and ever will, the one who created you. Knowing you are loved by the ultimate lover should put a smile on your face and a spring in your step.

Earlier when I said "don't give up, keep on looking," well, I went to a nail shop one day to get a fill in for my nails and I saw all of these people coming into the shop. I thought this shop must be the boom. So as I was waiting to be seen and was told to go and sit at this man's booth and he would do whatever I wanted done. Lo and behold, he messed my nails up. So one day I was riding and I saw another shop and I decided to go and see what they would do. As I walked in, the person at the first booth said, "What can I do for you?" I told him what I wanted done and he said to me, "I can do that for you."

When I sat down and he saw my nails, he asked, "Who did this mess?" So I explained it to him. He said, "I will fix it for you." What a great job he did. That is why I said don't give up, keep looking. You will find what you are looking for. He fixed my nails and made my nails look brand new. I went back three weeks later for my nails and my feet and I never had anyone out of my marriages to treat my feet the way he did. So if I had given up, I never would have found this person. I plan to get my feet taken care of as often as I can. He told me when I get ready to close my book to write about my treatment. And I did just that. Someone like that, you would be glad to recommend someone to them. That's one way of helping people to promote their business.

I hope my book will be a blessing to whoever reads it so they can tell someone else about it and will buy it for themselves. All I am trying to do is encourage people never to give up on their dreams. I will never forget what my late cousin told me. He said, "A winner never quits and a quitter never wins." I believe God said we are more than a conqueror; we are victorious. I have always said if I can't have the best, I don't want the less. But we never know what the outcome will be in whatever we get. I can truly say, if you have Jesus you have the best. That is why I am at peace and feel like I can run on and see what the end will be. I believe the Bible said, "And let us not be weary in well doing: for in due season we shall reap, if we faint not" (Galatians 6:9 KJV).

Conclusion

I have concluded that when the Bible says "a lot is called but a few are chosen," the chosen one has to go through more than the one that is called. That is why we have to go through so much because God knows who can and who can't take what we have to go through to be able to stand. I was reading in the book of Exodus 13:17-22, when Pharaoh let the people go, God did not lead them on the road through the Philistine country though that was shorter. Instead, He sent them on the hard road through the desert. In the short run, this helped them avoid wars; but in the long run, there was something bigger at work.

God used that time in the desert to instruct and mature the people. He had called to follow Him. The easy road would have led them to disaster. The long road prepared the nation of Israel for their successful entry into the Promised Land. Our God is faithful and we can trust Him to lead us and care for us no matter what we face. We may not understand the reason for the path we are on, but we can trust Him to help us grow in faith and maturity along the way.

Lord, we cannot see the path ahead so we must trust that the way is right and that it is the best road for us to take. Please encourage us and teach us as we let you direct our path. God's timing is always right; wait patiently for Him. I am so glad I waited on God and heard his voice when He told me I could get out of the marriage I was in. I followed His path and He directed me into the Promised Land. Now I can run, now I can have faith and know there are better things waiting for me.

I heard God say when He called me in 1975, "Upon this rock I will build my church and the gates of hell shall not prevail against it." In other words, mess with it if you want to and see what will happen to you. Being chosen is a wonderful thing. That way, you know God got you all the way. The songwriter said "When I think of the goodness of Jesus and all He has done for me, my Soul cries out; I thank God for saving me."

Acknowledgements

Here's to all those who work tirelessly to help make me be a better writer, encouraged me to dig deeper, and to remind me to keep it real.

To Christian Faith Publishing: Ms. Marie Rizo and others, who continue to support me and encourage me to keep sharing from the word and from my heart. I couldn't do this without you. You will always be in my heart and I will pray for the time you put in helping me. To God be the glory.

To My Best Friends

Apostle and prophetess Ola Foster, a person of great faith and always encouraging me to stay strong and hang on in there. She always says, "You can do it, you know you can. I have confidence in you, in the work that you do and always encourage me. That is why I know you can do it." She said, "I can't wait to read it. I enjoy talking with her; she is an inspiration to me and my ministry."

We have been working together for a number of years and never made no difference to each other in our lifestyle. Only one thing, when Apostle Foster met me, she told her husband I was a strange woman. Her husband told her, "But she

is a saved woman." We always laugh about that
when we see each other.

Ms. Parks

We met at Walnut Creek Elementary School in
2015 and have been friends ever since. She is a
substitute teacher and so am I. We love our job.
And most of all, we love the children. They help us
and we help them. Ms. Parks is a very sweet
person and our spirits clicked when we met.

Biography of Apostle Rev. Dr. Florene Vick Jones

Apostle Rev. Dr. Florene Vick Jones was born to the late Cleveland and Leora Vick in Zebulon, North Carolina. She is one of eight children. Dr. Jones was called into the ministry in 1975 and has been diligently and faithfully spreading the word of God. She received her Master in Ministries of Arts in May 2009, and in May 2013 she received her Doctorate Degree in Biblical Studies from Justice Fellowship College International. Dr. Jones also has her Chaplain Degree from Johnston Community College.

She has three beautiful children: Annette Jones Bullock, Cleveland Mclinton Jones, and Stephanie Renee Jones Williams. Dr. Jones also works as a substitute school teacher in the Wake County Public School.

Doctor Jones has a family reunion that was started by her in 1976 and has been going on ever since. As of July 17, 2010, we made it through our 32nd year! God has been good to Dr. Jones. She has an Affiliation of Churches she corresponds with such as Crusaders Holiness Church, Good Samaritan Baptist Church, Free Spirit Missionary

Baptist Church, Pentecostal Holiness Church, Pleasant Hill Holiness Church, All Faith Baptist Church, God Is Real Holiness Church, New Jerusalem Holiness Church, Solid Rock Holiness Church, Cornerstone Holiness Church, and Crusader International Church of God.

Apostle Rev. Dr. Florene Jones is just an all-around woman who loves people. She works faithfully with Alpha and Omega Outreach Ministries located at 2412-B Paula Street, Raleigh, North Carolina 27608 with the leadership of Apostle Ned Lee Mclean.

About the Author

Apostle Rev. Dr. Florene Jones pastors at her own church for more than twenty-four years. She received her Master Degree in Ministry Of Arts in 2009, and May 2013 received her Doctorate Degree in Biblical Studies from Justice Fellowship College International. She also has a Chaplain Degree from Johnson Community College. She retired from Rex Hospital in 1995. In 2014, she started working as a Substitute School teacher in Wake County Public Schools. On August 11th, she received her certificate for 20.0 hours foe Certified Substitute Teacher.

www.ingramcontent.com/pod-product-compliance
Lightning Source LLC
Chambersburg PA
CBHW051335120626
46547CB00016B/2548